Sixty–Three Years

February 1, 1958 – February 5, 2021

Carolyn Arrowood Harrod–George Ross Harrod

Carolyn Harrod

Parson's Porch Books

Sixty–Three Years
ISBN: Softcover 978-1-955581-83-7
Copyright © 2022 by Carolyn Harrod

Parson's Porch Books is an imprint of Parson's Porch & Company (PP&C) in Cleveland, Tennessee. PP&C is an innovative organization which raises money by publishing books of noted authors, representing all genres. Its face and voice is **David Tullock** (dtullock@parsonsporch.com).

Parson's Porch & Company *turns books into bread & milk* by sharing its profits with the poor.

www.parsonsporch.com

Sixty-Three Years

February 1, 1958 - February 5, 2021

Carolyn Arrowood Harrod -- George Ross Harrod

Our Earthly Journey Completed
Eternity in Heaven Yet to Come

"I Love You, Ross"

Dedicated to the Memory

Of My Sweet Husband, Ross

Who waits for me on the other side

Whether in Birmingham, Atlanta, Spartanburg, Chattanooga, Macon, Columbus, Mayfield, or Etowah, Ross and I enjoyed many walks together, often in a brisk march-like style. We kept in step as Ross' dynamic voice resounded with traditional marching chants which I suppose reflected his time in the Military.

Sound Off!

July 10, 1991

I n the eve when day is done,
We go walkin', we have fun;
Sounding cadence as we go,
Hup and two and three and fo'
…hup, hup, hup…

"Lift your feet and lift them high,
You can do it if you try."
All the neighbors think that we
Must have fallen off a tree.
…two, three, four…

Every car goes by we greet,
But we do not slow our feet;
If you happen on our way,
We bid you a lovely day.
…your left, your left…

Little creatures that we pass
Scamper through the rustling grass;
Of our step they are afraid,
They don't mess with this parade.
...and then your right...

First the left and then the right
Are we going to tramp all night?
Surely we have been a mile,
Can't we rest a little while?
...your right, your right...

"Not just yet," I hear him say,
"We've just started on our way;
If the going should get rough,
 A little more will make you tough."
...left, right, left, right...

We march on, I keep in stride,
Trusting him to be my guide:
I love him and he loves me,
We're a happy company.
...hup, hup, hup, hup...

As we tread the road of life,
Glad am I to be his wife;
With his love to show the way,
By his side I'll ever stay.
...hup, hup, hup... Sound Off!

Reprint from *Critters in the House*
Carolyn Arrowood Harrod, Copyright 2012

Sixty-Three Years

February 1, 1958 – February 5, 2021

H ow beautiful, and how frightening are the days of young adulthood. It is a time of insecurity and promise. The future is ours for the taking. The decisions which are made during these formative years affect the entire course of our lives and cannot be undone. My decision to become a Christian when I was embarking on life's journey in my teens was the best decision I have ever made, and positively influenced all other decisions which presented themselves during this difficult time. I not only strove to pursue Christian values, which led to making worthwhile decisions, but whereas I had previously felt a great sense of inadequacy,

I now felt that in God's sight I was valued, and that alone mattered.

I also felt that within me I had been gifted with a guiding presence leading me in the right direction if I listened and complied. I truly believe that this presence led me toward the selection of my life's companion, and sixty-three years of a beautiful marriage. My dear husband departed from his earthly existence this past February 5, 2021, just four days past our sixty-third anniversary, but I feel that his spirit is with me still, and that one day we will be together again in the presence of God. This writing is about some of the challenges I faced as a young Christian leading up to the time that I met and married the one God intended for me.

My parents loved me and taught me to love – a truth I only came to fully appreciate in much later years. My teenage years were a difficult time for all of us. Daddy worked nights, whether well or sick, and got whatever sleep he could in the daytime. With two young daughters who had joined our family group of four, I imagine he rarely got sufficient rest. I had a younger brother, but I had always wanted a sister. Now I found myself with two, the first born when I was fifteen, and the second when I was seventeen. I loved them both, and they loved me in return, and looked upon me as a second mother. When I began working before, and after high school graduation, I bought them shoes, special clothes at Easter, toys at Christmas, took them for walks when I came home from school, or work, often gave them their baths at night, prepared bottles, and sang to them at bedtime. My brother did his part as well. We had no time for the role of the carefree, and sometimes rebellious teenager which is often considered to be an expected part of these growing-up years.

As a new Christian, I felt the strength-giving need of attending church services, and I often took my little sisters with me. In fact, when the one God had chosen for me first felt an attraction to me as he spotted me sitting a few rows ahead of him in church, I had two little girls with me, so he thought I must have a husband somewhere. He later said that it was the happiest moment of his life when he learned that these children were my sisters, and that I was not married, but more about that later.

Daddy and his younger sister had been reared by their grandparents in Dayton, Tennessee, after the death of their mother during the birth of her third child. Daddy's parents had earlier left Dayton to hopefully prove a parcel of land in Billings, Montana through a government land grant. Following the death of his wife, Daddy's father brought Dad and his little sister back to their grandparent's home in Dayton, and only returned one more time to visit them. He later remarried, had a second family, and spent the remainder of his life in Montana.

Daddy's grandfather was a highly respected, and much-loved elder, as well as preacher at the Dayton Church of Christ.

Daddy had once been a faithful Christian and was the song director at the church we attended in East Gadsden, Alabama before our move to the big city of Birmingham. Mother had grown up in the Baptist Church but had become a member of the Church of Christ when she and Daddy married. Daddy and Mother attended the Central congregation of the Church of Christ in Birmingham a few times, and my brother and I were baptized here. Mother and Daddy never felt comfortable in this much larger congregation, however, and after the birth of two more children, life's demands became too heavy for either Mother or Daddy to include church.

In fact, they had very little social life of any sort as far as I know. Daddy held an amateur radio operator license, and he enjoyed this and related pursuits of radio electronics in whatever time he could find between work and sleep. For Mother, the days were consumed with the care of two young children in a house with a long flight of stairs separating the kitchen from the upstairs living room, bedrooms, and only bathroom. Daddy slept in the daytime in a bed/sitting room adjoining the kitchen. This room was heated by keeping a fire in the fireplace in cold weather, but the house was mainly heated in the winter by the maintenance of a fire in a huge stove in the kitchen. Wire covered square openings in the floors of two of the bedrooms above allowed heat to rise for warmth in these rooms. These bedrooms had fireplaces but had been closed off before we became tenants of this house. The living room and the third bedroom also had fireplaces, and fires were built in the living room during the winter months, and were sometimes built in the third bedroom, as well. It took continual effort to keep the house warm when the weather became cold.

Daddy worked diligently to provide for his family. As a young, insensitive adult, I once said to Mother that money had always seemed to be a problem for her and Daddy, and she replied that yes, there had never seemed to be enough of it to go around. I remember when the finance company employee came and towed away our car for lack of payment obligation. I happened to be home the day that the power company representative came to turn off our electricity for the same reason, and I told the guy that the bill would be paid right away. Apparently I was convincing because he left the power on. I remember that Mother seemed very embarrassed and, I'm sure, concerned for her family's wellbeing without electricity, and I felt very protective toward her. There was never anything extra for her or Daddy for personal pleasure during this time.

We rented our house, which was reputed to be over a hundred years old, and was isolated on a graveled road, and centered amidst back doors of other houses in every direction, from a family at church. I felt so belittled the day the owners came by to check on their property, and possibly to secure rent payment which may have been in arrears. The husband went inside the house to speak with Mother and Daddy, and the lady did not even get out of the car. I was alone outside when she spoke in a negative, and condescending manner. She made accusation that it looked like a fire had been built under the oak tree in the front yard. I don't know if this was true or not, or whether the tree had suffered damage, but I know that I was caused to feel undeserved guilt, and a great sense of condemnation.

This was a most difficult time for our family, but through it all we bound together and looked out for each other. When I began working, I had a telephone installed, and this was helpful with communication between each other, as well as with Mother's family in Tennessee. These were lean times, for sure, but the good far outweighed the bad. We had food, shelter, and transportation in one form or another. With two babies growing into toddlers, then young children, there was always joy in watching them learn to walk, talk, and grow in awareness about the world around them.

I received a set of Samsonite luggage as a gift from my parents when I graduated from high school, and I decided to take a vacation from work and go to Dayton to visit with my cousins, aunts, and uncles of Mother's family. I asked for permission to take my older baby sister with me, and permission was readily given. My sister, who was three years old at the time claimed the smaller of my luggage set and looked forward to riding on the 'Doggie' bus (Greyhound). We changed buses successfully in Chattanooga with my holding tightly to her little hand and arrived safely in Dayton. This was a vacation long to be remembered by me as being mostly a babysitter for my little sister. She was a very active child, and every waking moment was spent looking out for her welfare, but I loved her, and relish the memory of this special time with her. I'm sure Mother got a well-deserved rest.

Our family also had visits from Dayton, some of which lasted a week, or longer. My Dad's sister and her husband stayed with us for several weeks during their relocation from Dayton to Birmingham. Following the death of Mother's father, my Grandmother often came and helped Mother with the care of my little sisters. Mother also made friends with several neighbors, and they were in and out of our house. I remember that one older neighbor even spent the night at our house one time when she was to be left alone. She got up during the night to go to the bathroom, became confused about the location of her bedroom as she returned to bed, came into my bedroom instead, and startled me as she attempted to get into my bed. She realized her mistake and apologized with embarrassment.

Yes, there were good times, as well, and I have many fond family-related memories of my teenage years!

My decision to become a Christian certainly directed the course of my life. I always attended church services, riding the bus during daylight times, and hiring a taxi for Sunday evening and Wednesday evening, when it would be dark. I remember one time that the taxi was late, and as most of the other church attendees had already left, I had the fear of being left alone at the downtown church building at night, but that did not happen. After a time, my Sunday-School teacher and his wife provided my transportation home from church in the evenings. I remember that my brother, also, often rode the bus with me to church, and later, when he got a driver's license and purchased a car provided our transportation to church, and when, after my high-school graduation I attended the University of Alabama Extension in Birmingham at night, he was working nearby, and often provided my transportation home.

I still remember some of the sermons I heard during this time. One, which greatly inspired me was about doing one's best in every undertaking, as if the task is for the Lord (Col. 3:23). I took this message to heart, from henceforth tried to go beyond the sense of duty, or expectation, and was blessed with scholastic success at school, and later continuously increasing pay raises at work up until the time I left my job to be married and move to another state. In putting forth greater effort in school, and by completing assignments, my grades improved, and I began to realize that I was about as smart as anyone else, and perhaps smarter than some, because I now realized that the key to going forward in a positive manner was doing one's best. God had provided me with intelligence, but it had taken me awhile to learn how to use it.

I enrolled in the Diversified Occupations Program during my last two years of high school, which provided me with financial independence from my family, and allowed me to be helpful to my family's needs in some small ways. My brother, who had maintained paper routes from the age of twelve, also helped as he could. A turning point in my life was entering a Diversified Occupations essay contest which was offered, and in which students of the program were encouraged to take part. As I walked the halls from class to class soon after, I began receiving congratulations before I even realized that my essay had taken first place in the high school I attended. It later took first place in all the Birmingham schools, and I was provided with transportation to, and attendance at the Diversified Occupations State Convention in Montgomery, Alabama. My essay only took second place in the state but received publicity which reached out as far as to some of my relatives in Dayton, and I received congratulations here, as well. I was awarded a silver medal and felt a renewed sense of self-confidence. I later had the medal placed on a silver chain, and often wore it during times of low self-esteem.

Another sermon which had a strong impact on my life was that no matter how insignificant one may consider oneself, there is always someone looking to you for guidance and inspiration (I Tim. 4:12). I realized that I had a great responsibility toward my little sisters. Now, I understood that others, as well looked up to me for inspiration. My family had moved to Birmingham the year I started high school, and everybody was new to me. I did, however, make acquaintances with a few from my neighborhood, school, church, and later from work, and I feel we inspired each other in special ways.

Through my enrollment in the Diversified Occupations Program I attended school one half day and worked a half day. This meant that I only took business courses in high school and was not able to take college preparatory classes. It had been my earnest desire to go to college, and a favorite teacher told me to hold on to this dream, and that one day it would be fulfilled. I never ceased yearning for more education, and after graduating from Phillips High School in 1953, I eventually received the Bachelor of Arts degree in Music with emphasis on piano performance from the University of Tennessee at Chattanooga in 1979. My dear husband understood how much this meant to me, and after our marriage, and children had become of school age, he encouraged me to follow my dream.

My half-day job during high school was as a typist for a Certified Public Accountant in downtown Birmingham. I walked several blocks each school day from Phillips to my job. The sermon I had heard about doing one's best was certainly put to the test here. This was a time before computerized erasures, and whatever was typed remained unless manually erased. As I typed legal documents with columns of figures, no erasures were permitted. The pay was not great, and when, after high school graduation I was offered a much higher paying position at a large aircraft company in the Birmingham area, I accepted. I was now nineteen, and it would be about three more years before I made the second biggest decision of my life, that of beginning the journey toward sixty-three years of a beautiful marriage.

But now was my time of relative independence. I still lived in my parents' home, but they had long ago trusted me to make my own decisions, and never questioned my coming and going. I earned a reasonably good wage at my job and was able to help at home to a small degree, take care of personal needs and wants, make church contributions, and deposit a portion into a savings account each payday. It was still my desire to go to college, and David Lipscomb University in Nashville, Tennessee was my school of choice. I must confess here that I hoped to be able to save enough to provide an entrance into this school, meet and marry a missionary student, and help spread the gospel with him in foreign lands. This was not to be, but a future much more suitable and fulfilling awaited me.

In the meantime, I enrolled at the University of Alabama Extension in Birmingham in the evenings after working all day at my job. Transportation to the school after work, then on home after classes presented challenges. There was also little time for study, and although my grades were A's and B's, except for one C in Political Science, by the grace of the teacher, I became discouraged, and at the time lost enthusiasm for this effort. I did, however, accrue several first-year college credits.

I did not date at all during high school and dated very little during this time. I do have a fond remembrance, however, of calling home from work one day, and Mother telling me that I had received mail from a college address. I could hardly wait to get home that evening. It was from a young man who was in my Sunday School Class asking me to go out with him when he came home from school the following weekend. I accepted, and we had a nice evening out, but that was it. We did not share an attraction for each other. He later married another young lady from church, and as far as I know they have had a good marriage.

I also dated a young man who was
introduced to me by a girlfriend at church.
This young man had a hearing deficiency,
but we were able to communicate when I
looked in his direction when speaking so
that he could read my lips. I enjoyed the
quietness and peace in visits to the home of
some of his friends who only spoke in sign
language. There seemed to be a strong
sense of warmth and love here. He
attended some of the musical productions
in which I took part, and made pictures of
the scenes I was in, which I still treasure. I
enjoyed several Sunday afternoons with
him, but there was no strong attraction
here, and after a time we parted. I hope he
later found someone suitable for him.

I also once dated a college friend of
the manager of the office in which I worked.
He was a very nice young man, and I liked
him, but shortly after our first date, I met
the one I knew was God's intended for me.
I created quite a stir in the office when I
was asked out the second time by this
young man, and I said no, because I was

seeing someone else. He asked if we were engaged or 'going steady,' and I said no, but I did not intend to go out with anyone else. No words of a permanent significance had transpired between my future life's partner and me at this time, but I felt within my heart that he was the one God had in mind for me.

During this time of my personal independence I took several memorable vacation trips with friends from work and church. One interesting weekend automobile trip from Friday afternoon after work until late Sunday evening to New Orleans and back was spent with several young ladies from work. I greatly enjoyed the daytime tours on Saturday, and innocently began the night-club tour with my friends. At the first stop, when the young performer began to conduct herself in a provocative manner, I realized that this was not where I wanted to be, so I left my fellow travelers and returned by taxi to the hotel where we were staying. As I left the bleacher-type spectator seats in my departure from the event, it was necessary for me to walk along the edge of the stage as I made my way to the door. My eyes, and those of the performer met briefly, and I later wondered if that was not where she wanted to be, either, but was a matter of seeming necessity.

Back at the hotel I had a good night's rest, and the next morning arose and took a taxi for worship at the New Orleans Church of Christ. The church was so friendly that I almost regretted that I could not stay and attend more services there. When I returned to the hotel I was a bit disappointed to learn that we were packing up to leave. I felt refreshed, but the others seemed tired after having been out to the early morning hours the night before.

I also traveled by bus with two friends from church for a week's vacation to Jacksonville Beach, Florida. This provided my first spectacular view of the Atlantic Ocean. I was awed by its vastness! There was water as far as the eye could see out to the horizon. I was truly impressed by this wonder of God's creation. With these friends, there was no question of whether we would attend church. We did and met two young men there who offered to take us to lunch, and then to a tour of Hialeah Racetrack. We spent a most enjoyable Sunday afternoon with these kind, and most hospitable gentlemen.

I am now approaching the time of my meeting God's intended for me, but first, a brief interlude as I recount my confused rejection of the one I *thought* was my intended. It came about in this way. When I was twenty-two, two of my friends from church and I decided to travel on vacation to Nassau in the Bahamas. Well, wonder of wonders, the nephew of the president of the large company for which I worked, and was tall, good-looking, and *very* eligible declared that he, too, was planning to accompany his mother and his aunt to Nassau at the same time as I. He advised me about flights and where to stay, so that our travel and hotel accommodations would coincide. Was this not fate! He was a very nice person with Christian values. I liked him, and I really looked forward to getting better acquainted with him in Nassau!

But something happened that I could not explain at the time. The presence within me, which always seemed to serve as my guide, seemed to reject, and to guard against any closeness which may have developed between us. I found myself dismissing any opportunity that was offered to get to know him better. It seemed to be beyond my control, but for some mysterious reason I never allowed myself to be alone with him, but always insisted upon the presence of my girlfriends when advances were made for personal time together.

When I returned home from vacation I thought, *"What have I done?"* I was devastated and felt a great sense of opportunity lost. I even considered calling him and apologizing, but thankfully, I did not. Only a short time later I understood why my inner being had forbidden a possible life-time relationship with this young man. I hoped he later found someone suitable for him, but I was being saved for someone else! The decision which I later made to join my life with that of this 'someone else' made all the difference. I *knew* that he was a Christian, and he was also a member of the Church of Christ, as was I.

Our meeting was like this. Shortly after my return from Nassau, my intended responded to the Invitation one Sunday morning to place his membership at the church I attended. That evening, the young, single adults planned to go to Shoney's after the service, and it was suggested that this new church member be invited, but who was to extend the invitation. Somehow it happened that I would have the honor. I did, he accepted, and offered to provide transportation for me and the friend who was with me when he was invited. He also suggested that we all three sit up front so that no one would be alone in the back or the front of the car. Again, it was to be determined who would sit in the middle. I somehow found myself being prodded into the seat beside him, and my girlfriend taking the outside seat by the window.

At Shoney's, he asked me about my children. I did not understand at first, then I realized he was referring to my little sisters. I have already mentioned that he later told me that these were the sweetest words that he had ever heard. *I was not married!*

I again sat beside him as he took me home that evening, and I have been beside him ever since, until this past February, but I still feel his spiritual presence, and look forward to being with him again in Heaven one day, as we spend eternity together. We met the last Sunday of October 1957, and were joined together in marriage on February 1, 1958, just about three months later. This time my inner being told me

"*YES*! This is the one God has in mind for you," and I listened!

The greatest decision I made in my young adulthood which directed the course of my life was becoming a Christian, and the second most important decision was waiting for, and responding to the dictates of my inner being when it came to the choice of a life's companion.

My dear husband passed away this past February fifth, just four days after we had celebrated sixty-three years of marriage, but I am left with many beautiful memories. Our time together on earth has ended, but I feel he is with me still. Sometimes I even sense his arm around me as I lie in bed at night, and I remember how that each night toward the end of his life he always told me that he loved me, that I was the most beautiful woman in the world, then would correct himself and say, "No, the *only* beautiful woman in the world!" He would then tell me how that he was the most blessed man in the world to have me as his wife, and that if I needed anything during the night to call him. These words became so repetitive each night, I regret to remember that I sometimes thought to myself, 'Yeah, yeah, I know what you are going to say next.' I now understand the meaning of this repetition. He knew his end was soon to come, and he wanted to leave me with a positive assurance of his love.

I am truly blessed with beautiful memories of sixty-three years spent with the one God led to me. God brought us together after my intended had fulfilled his patriotic duty in the army, had received the Bachelor of Industrial Engineering degree from Georgia Tech, and had accepted a responsible position with the Southern Railroad. This job brought him to Birmingham and membership in the Central Church of Christ just long enough for us to meet. Two weeks before our wedding his job took him to Atlanta, Georgia, but he returned for our wedding, and we were joined together in marriage at the Central Church of Christ on February 1, 1958 and faced our future as husband and wife. We have supported each other through the desire, and pursuit of natural-born children, then the later adoption of two beautiful babies and the resultant family life thereafter; my acquiring a college degree; job changes and relocations which once involved five major moves in five years with contracts on the sale of two houses and the purchase of a third one in three different states.

I did not marry a missionary, but before we married my husband-to-be told me that he felt we could serve God together, and after departing this earthly existence have a home with Him in Heaven. My loved one has gone on before. I miss him, but I am comforted by the promise of our reunion when my time comes to join him for eternal bliss.

My husband and I were faithful church attendees throughout our life together, and often served as Sunday School and Vacation Bible School teachers.

In the early years of our marriage, we worked with, and planned activities for the youth of the church. My husband once served as a deacon, and later served as an elder of the church we attended while living in Chattanooga. Following his retirement, we relocated to Athens, Tennessee to help with the care of his aging mother, and soon after he began serving as an elder of the Athens Church of Christ. He was still serving in this capacity at the time of his passing.

Along with our choice of parenthood, we have each served as Scout leaders, and my husband was the coach of winning Little League baseball teams for several years.

Yes, I am left with beautiful memories, but I also am blessed with the promise of a continuance of our life together one day in Heaven. I look forward to seeing him again, and to saying 'Thank You' to the presence who came to live within me when I became a Christian for guiding the course of my life. I would like to write that I have always chosen wisely, but I am not perfect. According to scripture, perfection is a state toward which we strive (Phil. 3:12-14), and I am not there yet. I am thankful, however, that my dear husband and I were able to serve God, and to love and support each other throughout our sixty-three years of marriage, that our children, including our sweet daughter-in-law are Christians, and that our grandson is growing up in a Christian home.

I am most thankful, however, that I obeyed God's direction to become a Christian, and to wait patiently for the one He had chosen to become my life's partner. I miss him so, but I look forward to our spending eternity together in the presence of Him who knew our need for each other, and so directed our paths.

If Only

October 31, 2021

I did not know but should have known
That I would soon be left alone
To mourn the loss of the one I love,
Who left me for his home above.

He told me plain that he would die,
And I replied, "Well, so will I –
So will we all, as God has said,
But not just yet, that's far ahead."

I could not accept that for my mate
The time had come to meet his fate.
If only I could have wept back then,
And expressed my love again and again.

I miss him so – great is my pain,
But one day soon we'll meet again,
And I know, Lord, that he's with You.
Please hold him close till I come too!

Y O U

October 2021

I saw you today – or at least I thought I did, and in that moment I felt the peace and joy that was once a familiar part of my life, so much so, that perhaps it was not fully recognized, and appreciated.

I had pulled into a parking space in front of Dollar General and was preparing to enter the store when I looked up and saw you approaching the car, returning to where I waited while you made your purchases.

I could only see a partial view of your midsection through the front windshield as you approached, but I knew it was you. I recognized the khaki pants and maroon-colored dress shirt which you often wore. Your shirt was neatly tucked into your pants, and your dark one-inch leather belt encircling your trim, but masculine waist neatly bound them together.

In that moment I was transported back in time, and eagerly awaited your return to the car to ask if you found everything you wanted. But then the gentleman came into full view ------- and it wasn't you.

I cried - - - - - - -

DREAMS

I was awoken to the sound of my own voice crying out for help. In my dream I had been walking beside the windowless brick wall of the drugstore about my parent's home where I lived before my marriage. The street was deserted, as it often was when I exited the city bus at this drugstore at night, returning home from work or school.

A man was approaching me from across the street. I knew the man was intent on evil, but I was not afraid. I just knew that I needed help. And so I cried out again, and again – hoping to be heard.

As I awoke from this threatening dream, I was concerned that my cry for help would cause others in the house to rush to my bedroom to see what was wrong, and I would have to explain that it was just a dream. Then I realized that there *was* no one else in the house, and the house never felt so empty.

The next night in my dream I composed the rhyming first lines of the poem I have entitled *PEACE*. I was singing it to the tune of *This Is My Father's World* when I awoke. The next day, and several days thereafter the remaining lines came into my mind. I feel this poem was given me through inspiration to remind me that I am in God's care.

I feel that the tune of the song to which I was singing the first lines of the poem in my sleep is also significant. The hymn, *This Is My Father's World* reminds me that God is in control, and through love and trust in Him there is no place for fear. I John 4:18 tells me that 'Perfect love casts out fear.'

The tune to which I was singing in my sleep belongs to another, but the words of the poem are original with me through inspiration and are a special blessing from God. The silent recitation of this poem has often brought me *Peace*.

PEACE

July 2021

I know my God is good,
He keeps me in His care.
When I'm alone and feel afraid,
For me He is always there.

He tells me in His Book
That I should trusting be,
And then one day with Him I'll live
Forever in eternity.

How long, O Lord, how long
Till I Thy face may see?
The days are lonely for me now,
And I would come to Thee.

Wait patiently, My child
For others need you still.
When days are long, I'll see you through.
I always have, --- Always will.

A reprisal of the thoughts of each verse later came to mind, along with an accompanying melody.

Peace with Reprise

January 15, 2022

I know my God is good.
He keeps me in His care.
When I'm alone and feel afraid,
For me He is always there.

God keeps me in His care,
Whatever may prevail.
Through doubt and fear, He is always near.
His love for me shall never fail.

He tells me in His book
That I should trusting be,
And then one day with Him I'll live
Forever in eternity.

I'll trust in Him each day,
Let come whatever may.
He is my guide, there is none beside
Can banish all my cares away.

How long O Lord, how long
Till I Thy face may see?
The days are lonely for me now,
And I would come to Thee.

In loneliness I sigh.
Take me home Lord is my cry.
There's naught I see left of joy for me.
It's only in Thee do I rely.

Wait patiently My child,
For others need you still.
When days are long, I'll see you through.
I always have, --- Always will.

I'll wait for Thee, O Lord,
For I know You will afford
Strength only You have to see me through
Till Heaven shall be my reward.

PEACE

Carolyn Harrod

PEACE—4-Part Harmony

Carolyn Harrod

A Rare Conflict

Ross and I had a good marriage. He was always my towering strength and sought to provide for me in every way. He often told me he loved me, and how that he was blessed to have me as his wife. I know I was truly blessed to have him for my husband. I feel that God must have worn a big smile of satisfaction when He brought us together. In sixty-three years of marriage, however, there were bound to have been occasional conflicts, but nothing that deeply shook the bedrock of our love for each other.

One such incident which I will herewith relate centered around my fear of heights. I knew that a trip to Alaska would probably encounter heights, but this was a life-time dream for Ross and appealed to me as well. I just tried to lay aside my concern about heights and focus on the adventure.

Well, of course, inevitably the heights –and depths– of Alaska quickly made themselves known. Most of the time I just closed my eyes, got very quiet, and tried to not make an issue of my discomfort. On one occasion, however, I was not able to hide my fear. I loved Ross with all my heart, but I absolutely could not bring myself to go on the White Pass Yukon train ride in Skagway, Alaska, which Ross had so looked forward to, and this is the rare conflict of which I am about to relate.

We had enjoyed a good breakfast at the Sweet Tooth Café in Skagway and were preparing to embark on the day's adventure when our son, David called on my cell phone. Perhaps if it had not been for the cumulative tiredness of the trip, and possibly the deprivation of sleep due to excessive snoring, I could have handled this

day better. Admittedly, I had been
apprehensive about this train ride since I
saw the video of it displaying the extreme
heights along the way as the train made its
way along the side of the mountain. But I
was determined to take the tour because I
knew Ross was looking forward to it. I also
felt that it must be safe because the tour
had been in operation for many years. As
earlier noted, however, I do have an
extreme sensitivity to heights that is
perhaps not easily understood. I was
fighting hard to overcome this deterrent,
but when I talked to David I was not able to
keep a tear from rolling down my cheek.

Unfortunately, Ross saw it, and
became angry with me. He embarrassed
me before our fellow travelers by saying
that if I was going to cry about it, we would
not go. I begged him to go without me. I
said that I could write postcards, do
laundry, shop, rest, etc., but he would not. I
felt devastated to have kept him from doing
something he wanted to do. The pain I felt
could hardly be endured. Ross got a refund

on our tickets, and my brother and sister-in-law boarded the train without us.

In his anger, or frustration, Ross said that I had been miserable for the whole trip, and that I had not had a good time. On the way back to the motel I experienced an asthmatic attack. Ross tried to sit beside me on the sidewalk bench where I had taken refuge, but I didn't want him near me. I felt so alone and felt that my 'unreasonable' fear of heights had not only ruined the day but had spoiled the remainder of the trip. My greatest pain came from the fact that I knew Ross had really wanted to take this train ride but was kept from it because of my weakness.

When we got back to the motel room, I tried to rest, but could not, so I did a lot of hand laundry. Ross looked at maps and went in and out of the motel room. The silence between us was almost unbearable. I knew this needed to be settled before my brother and sister-in-law returned, so I apologized for not having had the courage to decline the train ride from the beginning, so that we could have had more time to plan for Ross to go on it without me if he wanted to. I then came to the realization that I had the right to choose what I felt comfortable to do, and that I should not have tried to force myself otherwise. I realized also that Ross, too, had the right to choose to not go without me if that was his desire. Ross told me that he loved me and that I was more important to him than a train ride. I was very regretful that he missed the ride, but nothing could be done about it now, so I decided to let it go and try to get over it.

We walked about through the town of Skagway, browsed through several shops, then continued on to meet our fellow travelers at the end of their train ride. We were completely reconciled, and I felt greatly strengthened and secure once again in Ross' love for me.

Of course, there were further challenges ahead to face in this great

Alaskan adventure, including one bus trip around the side of the mountain at Denali which I was told by my sister-in-law was every bit as fearful as the White Pass Yukon train ride she and my brother had taken, but I had renewed strength and determination, and was able to face each new upcoming adventure with *almost* as much bravado as everyone else.

"The heavens declare the glory of God;
And the firmament shows His handiwork."
Psalm 19:1

"Lord, You have been our dwelling place in all generations.

Before the mountains were brought forth, Or ever You had formed the earth and the world, Even from everlasting to everlasting, You are God."
Psalm 90:1, 2

Weary Travelers

Toward the end of Ross' working career the creosote plant of which he was the manager closed due to environmental reasons, and we embarked on a whirlwind of job changes and relocations, resulting in five major moves in as many years. As mentioned earlier in this writing, at one point we found ourselves with contracts on the sale of two houses and the purchase of a third house in three different states. It was a time of major unrest, but also of great adventure. I once found myself complaining that I was looking forward to my home in Heaven, because it didn't seem that I was going to have one here.

It was a difficult time for both of us, as well as for our children, who were at that time both in college – Amy at David Lipscomb and later at Middle Tennessee State University, then finally earning the Masters' Degree in Art Education at the University of Tennessee in Knoxville. David moved along with us and attended whatever college was close by. He eventually graduated with a Bachelors' Degree in Marketing from Murray State University in Murray, Kentucky.

This period of unrest also offered the excitement of job interviews in which Ross and I were treated with great respect and were provided with excellent hotel accommodations and meals. Following one of these interviews Ross and I returned to our then home in Columbus, Mississippi, tired from the trip and fraught with decisions to be made. Perhaps the weariness of our travel created the following confusing situation as we lay in our bed, falling quickly into a deep sleep. I later recorded this in my writings, entitled *Weary Travelers*.

> "The clamor reverberated loudly from somewhere a long way off into the deep recesses of the night. An intruder! A thief come to steal away blissful, strength-restoring rest and sleep! I must investigate, but no, I cannot awaken. It must be a dream. Am I yet asleep? Why is my husband stirring? Is he having the same dream? We have traveled for so long, lain in so many beds.
>
> We need to be restored of mind and body. Is someone moving about within the room? It is a dream! Why can I not become wake?
> Are my eyes open? Do I see lace curtains covering the window?
>
> I hear a voice – "Where are we? Whose house are we in?" Does the voice come from within the room, or from the confines of my dreams? I do not answer immediately. I just

stare at the vaguely familiar curtains until finally I hear my voice reply aloud, "I don't know *where* we are!" My husband hears me and announces, "We're home!"

The clamor continues, but now that we are both fully awake it is recognized to be the urgent knocking on our outside bedroom door. It is our son, who had returned home from school, and had been inadvertently locked out."

The last several years of Ross' working career were filled with continual challenge, but we weathered the storms of constant upheaval together, and enjoyed many beautiful rainbows along the way. We never lacked for anything, except a place to call home. With reference to an earlier listed conversation with my mother, 'there was *always* enough of it to go around.' Our basic needs were sufficiently met, and we never had to touch our savings for retirement.

A huge stumbling block was the sale of our then home in Columbus, Mississippi, but the day finally arrived when we were able to sell it at a loss and move to our final home together in Etowah, Tennessee. Our pre-retirement journey was now complete, and we had been able to enjoy almost twenty-eight years in a place to call home, before Ross' departure for his heavenly abode almost a year ago at the time of this writing. This is the longest either of us has ever lived at the same location. Our Etowah home has often been filled with family, church, and local gatherings. We have truly enjoyed our life here, and the blessings of being a part of a fixed church family and friendly community. We have also had the freedom to enjoy numerous travels together.

Our earthly journey together is now in the past. The arms that once held me now lie in a personally selected beautiful coffin in a family plot at Cedar Grove Cemetery in Athens, Tennessee, the city of his birth. The headstone above bears both our names, with the final date of my departure yet to be inscribed, but the spirit of the one who made my life complete is now with God, awaiting for mine to come and be joined together as one, for all eternity.

"I miss him so -- great is my pain,
But one day soon we'll meet again.
And I know, Lord, that he's with You.
Please hold him close till I come too!"

Twilight

August 1982

The eve draws nigh and I'm content
To take mine ease with no lament;
Each precious hour I full have spent
With diligence unending.

I've held within a joyful treasure,
Abundant life in fullest measure;
No time I've giv'n to wanton leisure,
Tho oft my heart was rending.

To live, to do, to be, to know,
This was my purpose here below;
To seek for love and love bestow,
My tears and laughter blending.

I've oft been tried and put to test
And now I'm tired and need to rest.
Thank You, Lord, I've been so blest!
My soul is Heav'nward wending.

Reprint with editing from *Critters in the House*
Carolyn Arrowood Harrod, Copyright 2012

In Memory Of

George Ross Harrod

Date of Birth

October 21, 1931

Date of Death

February 5, 2021

Funeral Services

2:00 PM, Sunday, February 7, 2021

Chapel of Laycock Hobbs Funeral Home

Athens, Tennesse

Officiating

Minister Mark Littleton

Interment

Cedar Grove Cemetery
Athens, Tennessee

Services In Care Of

Laycock Hobbs Funeral Home
Athens, Tennessee

George Ross Harrod, age 89 of Etowah, passed away Friday, February 5, 2021 at his residence.

A native of Athens and current resident of Etowah he was the son of the late George and Lou Ella Elliott Harrod.

A graduate of McMinn County High School and later of Georgia Tech with a Bachelor of Industrial Engineering, he was a veteran of the US Army having served during the Korean War.

A faithful member of the Church of Christ he served as a Sunday School teacher, deacon, youth director and had served as Elder of East Brainard Church of Christ and was currently serving as Elder for the Athens Church of Christ.

He also served as a Cub Scout Leader while in Macon, GA.

He was a Little League Baseball Coach having coached the Bombers and the Twins while in Chattanooga. The Bombers won their division and tied for the league championship and the Twins also won their division and the league championship. Ross then coached the Allstar Team twice.

He was a former employee of Southern Railroad for 10 years and was retired from Southern Wood Piedmont after 23 years of service and following his retirement he moved back to Athens to care for his mother and was employed with H&R Block.

Survivors:

He celebrated 63 years of marriage to his dearly loved wife, Carolyn on February 1, 2021. He was a devoted father to Amy and David and his daughter-in-law Renee and was a loving Grandfather to his very special grandson, Ryan.

One sister and brother-in-law, Imogene and Bill Torbett.

Funeral Services will be 2:00 PM Sunday, February 7, 2021 in the chapel of Laycock-Hobbs Funeral Home with Minister Mark Littleton officiating. Interment will follow in Cedar Grove Cemetery. Active pallbearers will be members of the Athens Church of Christ.

The family will receive friends from 1-2 PM Sunday prior to the service at the funeral home. Those unable to attend may send condolences to www.laycock-hobbs.com/notices/George-Harrod. Laycock-Hobbs Funeral Home in Athens is in charge of the arrangements.

Messenger
102MSPC
Printed in U.S.A.

In Memory Of

George Ross Harrod

October 21, 1931 ~ February 5, 2021

Two decisions made in young adulthood led to sixty-three years of a beautiful marriage on earth, and the promise of Heaven beyond.

"I miss him so – great is my pain,
But one day soon we'll meet again.
And I know, Lord, that he's with You.
Please hold him close till I come too!"

2/1/1958 – 2/5/2021

 Carolyn Harrod, 87, resides in Etowah, Tennessee, and is a member of the Athens Church of Christ, where for many years she taught the 1st, 2nd, and 3rd Grade Sunday School Class. Carolyn was recently granted an honorary membership of the Thursday Music Study Club of Etowah, of which she has presented numerous programs, and has served in various offices, including the presidency for several terms. Carolyn is also the author of *Critters in the House*, which was self-published in 2012 and shared with family and friends.